I0147070

Melville Egleston

The Land System of the New England Colonies

Melville Egleston

The Land System of the New England Colonies

ISBN/EAN: 9783337036027

Printed in Europe, USA, Canada, Australia, Japan

Cover: Foto ©ninafisch / pixelio.de

More available books at **www.hansebooks.com**

JOHNS HOPKINS UNIVERSITY STUDIES

IN

HISTORICAL AND POLITICAL SCIENCE

HERBERT B. ADAMS, Editor

History is past Politics and Politics present History.—*Freeman*

FOURTH SERIES

XI-XII

The Land System of the New England Colonies

BY MELVILLE EGLESTON

BALTIMORE

N. MURRAY, PUBLICATION AGENT, JOHNS HOPKINS UNIVERSITY

November and December, 1886

COPYRIGHT, 1886, BY N. MURRAY.

ISAAC FRIEDENWALD, PRINTER,
BALTIMORE.

PREFATORY NOTE.

The following monograph was originally printed in the year 1880. Of the copies then issued some found their way at once into the larger public libraries, while others were placed in the hands of persons believed to be interested in the subject treated of. The number of these copies, however, all told, was quite small, and it was suggested some time ago by the editor of this series of "Johns Hopkins University Studies" that the results of the writer's investigations were not accessible to many to whom they might be useful, and that they were of sufficient interest to warrant their publication in the series named.

The opportunity courteously offered by him of reaching in this manner a greater number of persons interested in studies of the kind was gladly accepted, and the treatise is now reprinted, without any change whatever from the original form.

The author has deemed it important to make this explanatory statement, for nothing but the facts which have been mentioned could excuse, or even account for, the absence of reference to the numerous and valuable studies in the history of local institutions which have been published in this country during the past six years.

M. E.

NEW YORK, *November* 1, 1880.

THE LAND SYSTEM OF THE NEW ENGLAND COLONIES.

The laws of a State are the reflection of the economical and social condition of the people, while their form and spirit indicate the mental and moral status of those by whom the laws are made. They are thus among the most valuable and trustworthy sources of historical information which we possess. Especially is this the case where the people are themselves legislators. Yet the history of American legislation has not received the attentive study which it deserves, and which will surely some day be given to it. I have here subjected to examination a small portion of this interesting field. The close connection between the institution of land in any community and its political and social history is now well understood, and the importance of such an investigation as I have here undertaken will, I think, be recognized, however successful or unsuccessful the writer may be in his treatment of it.

I have endeavored to trace the origin and early history of our existing land system—a system than which none has yet been devised better suited to the conditions of any people. A complete presentation of the subject might well contain a fuller account of the laws of alienation and succession *ab intestato* than has been given ; but it seemed best for several reasons to consider them separately in another place. Enough has been given, however, for the present purpose, and the land system of New England was mainly determined by the legislation and customs here described.

In explaining the process by which the soil of New England was distributed among the occupants, I have followed what seemed to be the natural order, stating first the origin of rights in the land, and then describing successively each link in the chain of title, grants from the Crown, grants from the Great Council, colonial grants, and finally the division of lands among the members of the land communities. Local ordinances and recognized customs have been treated as important parts of the system.

I.

ORIGINAL SOURCES OF TITLE.

1.—RIGHT OF THE CROWN.

In the New England colonies all titles to landed property were derived originally from an actual or constructive grant of the English Crown. The title of the Crown itself was based upon that union of discovery and possession which, in the opinion of English jurists, could alone give a valid title to a new country. Mere transient discovery indeed amounted to nothing unless followed in a reasonable time by occupation more or less permanent under the sanction of the State.[1] But these conditions, it was held, had been fulfilled by the discovery of the coasts of America by the Cabots in the years 1497–8, and the subsequent visit of Sir Humphrey Gilbert in 1583, when he formally took possession of the country under letters-patent. Long as was the interval, it was in the eyes of England not too long, and that nation always based and maintained her claims to possessions in America upon the grounds here given.[2]

The rights of the Crown were not merely those of the head of a State, or of the feudal lord paramount. The King was the

---

[1] 3 Kent Comm. 380, n.
[2] *Ibid.*, and Thurlowe, State Papers.

immediate owner and lord of the soil, and exercised unlimited power in the disposition of it. He made grants which could not be made under English law, as, for instance, when he authorized the proprietaries of Maryland and other colonies to erect manors, " anything in the Statute of *'Quia emptores'* to the contrary notwithstanding."[1] He claimed also the right to establish local governments, and conferred powers of legislation upon his grantees, whether these were colonists in America or groups of courtiers in England. The rights of private ownership and royal prerogative were in him too closely combined to be readily distinguished.

2.—RIGHT OF THE ABORIGINES.

But although it was the theory of the British Government and of the colonists that the absolute, ultimate title to land was in the sovereign, that title was subject to a right of occupancy in the Indians. This natural right of the natives was entitled to protection; but the sole right of acquiring it by purchase or by actual conquest was in the Crown or its grantees, and the natives had no right to dispose of it to any other.[2]

The colonial governments uniformly acted upon these principles, so that, although individuals were disposed to deal less liberally with the natives, and even such a man as Cotton Mather deemed it unnecessary to recognize in any way their title,[3] the rights which the theory of the Government left to them received, as a rule, the protection required.

In Maine, owing to peculiar circumstances, the title conveyed by Indian deeds assumed especial importance, and a high degree of authority was accorded to such evidences of property. At about the time of the English Revolution, the colony of Massachusetts was striving vigorously to extend

---

Hazard, State Papers, I. 160, 327, 442, etc.
[2] 3 Kent, 379, etc.
[3] Magn. I. 72.

its boundaries, and, in order to weaken its enemy Gorges and render him unpopular, the colonial government supported the theory that the native right must be superior to that conferred by such an extensive patent as his. Purchases from the Indians, which in consequence became frequent and of great extent, were regularly upheld by the local courts.[1] When Massachusetts in 1716 appointed commissioners to record claims to lands, these Indian deeds were revived with other claims, and thus gained a standing as legal titles. The Government, however, became alarmed at their extent, and in 1731 passed an act forbidding all purchases from the natives without license of the Legislature, and declaring all deeds taken without such license to be null and void.[2]

This enactment was merely an extension to new territory of a policy already generally adopted in New England. Massachusetts herself had in 1633 passed a restrictive law applying to the territory then held by her.[3] Plymouth had done the same in 1643,[4] and Connecticut made similar regulations at an early date.[5]

That these laws were enforced is abundantly shown by the constant formal authorization of purchases,[6] as well as by the recorded cases of refusal to confirm purchases made without authority.[7] A grant of land, indeed, carried with it the right to extinguish the Indian title as of course, and no special authorization was needed. Yet even then, if the conditions of the grant were not fulfilled, the Government claimed the acquired title, if the planters had purchased.[8]

Not only was the necessity of acquiring the Indian title uniformly recognized, but in some cases, especially when be-

---

[1] Sullivan, Land Titles, 43.
[2] Acts and Res. of Mass. Bay.
[3] Mass. Rec., I. 112.
[4] Plym. Rec., Winslow's letter in Hazard, II. 531.
[5] Conn. Col. Rec., I. 214, 364, 402.
[6] Mass. Rec., II. 82, III. 225, etc.; Conn. Rec. I. 151, 418, 420, etc.
[7] *Ibid.* IV. 427, 430, 440, etc.
[8] *Ibid.* IV., Pt. II. 529.

yond the boundaries of an acknowledged local government, the colonists would seek no other titles, contenting themselves with that derived from the natives, without confirmation or authority from any other source. Roger Williams even took the ground that the planters could have no just title except what they derived from the Indians, in consequence of which heresy he was summoned before the court, and was also condemned by a council of ministers.[1] But in the settlement of Rhode Island his principles were strictly followed, and it is possible that no grant would have been sought there, except at the hands of the actual possessors of the soil, had not some formal authorization of their acts of self-government been found essential to safety. Parliamentary and royal grants were then obtained.

Connecticut was settled and its government organized without any charter or grant, and the lands were purchased by the planters from the Indians as they had need of them. Mr. Trumbull says, " The settlers of the river towns had not —before or after the agreement with Mr. Fenwick—any right of jurisdiction, except such as grew out of occupation, purchase from the native proprietors, or (in the case of the Pequot territory) of conquest." Their policy seems to have been to dispose as quietly and as cheaply as possible of the claims of such as challenged their title, into the exact nature of which they were not disposed to provoke too close an investigation.[2] But the General Court, as early as 1638, was given the sole power to "dispose of lands undisposed of," and regularly exercised the power.[3]

The titles to land in Nantucket and Martha's Vineyard originally were derived merely from Indian deeds, although the islands were soon placed under the jurisdiction of Massachusetts by the Congress of the United Colonies, and in 1692 were regularly incorporated by royal charter into the province

---

[1] Arnold, Hist. of R. I., I. 279.
[2] Conn. Rec., I. 569.
[3] *Ibid.* 25, etc.

of Massachusetts Bay.[1] Titles from the Crown were also acquired through the Earl of Stirling.

A careful examination of the records will satisfy a candid inquirer that there is no ground for materially modifying the statement of Chancellor Kent that "the people of all the New England Colonies settled their towns upon the basis of a title procured by fair purchase from the Indians with the consent of Government, except in the few instances of lands acquired by conquest after a war deemed to have been just and necessary."[2] Even where the title had been regularly acquired by purchase, the General Court of Massachusetts spoke of the native right as one "which cannot in strict justice be utterly extinct," and refused to dispossess the Indians, although it gave compensation in other lands to the town interested.[3]

II.

ROYAL GRANTS.

No fruitful attempts at colonization were made under the letters-patent granted to Gilbert, and after his death to his half-brother, Raleigh. But the zealous persistence of the latter, and the remarkable success of English merchants engaged in trading to distant lands—especially in connection with the operations of the famous Muscovy Company—prepared the minds of men for an enterprise in another quarter which promised great results, and, indeed, secured them, although not in the precise way expected. Gosnold's expedition in 1602, under the auspices of the Earl of Southampton, of which glowing reports were made by him and his companions on their return, was the immediate forerunner of a movement which resulted in the procurement of a charter,

---

[1] Sullivan, 38, 55.
[2] 3 Kent Comm. 391.
[3] Mass. Rec., IV. Pt. II. 49.

and the subsequent colonization of the coasts of America under the encouragement of its provisions.[1]

THE CHARTER OF 1606.[2]

The letters-patent issued in 1606 to Sir Thomas Gates and others granted to them the territories of America between 34° and 45° of north latitude, or from Cape Fear to Halifax, together with all islands within one hundred miles of their shores. The patentees were to divide themselves into two distinct companies, one of which, afterward called the London Company, was to have an exclusive right from 34° to 38° north, while the other, the Western, or Plymouth Company, was to have control between 41° and 45° north. The intermediate space was open to colonization by either. The London Company was dissolved by *quo warranto* in 1624. But it was not until 1635 that the Plymouth Company ceased to exist, and even then the surrender of its charter was voluntary.[3]

THE CHARTER OF 1620.[4]

Before any successful attempt at settlement had been made by the Plymouth Company, it was, with some changes of membership, made a separate body politic and corporate, under the name and style of "*The Council established at Plymouth, in the County of Devon, for the planting, ordering, ruling, and governing of New England in America.*"[5] The charter of 1620 granted to the new corporation certain territories, to be called New England, extending between 40° and 48° north latitude, and from sea to sea; to be held "as of the manor of East Greenwich in free and common socage." It gave

---

[1] Graham, Col. Hist. of the U. S., I. 44, etc.
[2] The Charter is in Hazard, State Papers, I. 50.
[3] Palfrey, Hist. of New England, I. 81–2, Hazard.
[4] Hazard, I. 103.
[5] Palfrey, Hist. of N. E., I. 192.

also rights of legislation and government; yet nothing came
of any attempts to exercise these rights, for deep hostility to
the patent was soon manifested, and from this, together with
other causes, the difficulties of the situation became so great
that the company in 1635 surrendered its charter to the
King.[1] It did not, however, do this until after making a
number of grants, which, from ignorance or carelessness as
to previous conveyances, and the want of accurate knowledge
of the geography of the country, were, in the words of Sullivan, "but a course of confusion."[2] Among these grants,
about which there has been so much dispute, were some of
importance, from the fact that through these is traced the
title to a great part of the soil of New England. These
grants will, therefore, be more particularly described here-
after.[3]

GRANT TO GORGES.

Another royal grant was made in 1639 to Sir Ferdinando
Gorges,[4] conveying a tract of land called the Province of
Maine, lying between the Piscataqua and the Kennebec, and
extending inland one hundred and twenty miles, from which
the whole State of which it is a part has taken its name.
All necessary powers of government were included in the
grant, and its tenure was in free and common socage. But
this grant was at an early date assailed by settlers, and
indirectly by the government of Massachusetts Bay, which,
in order to weaken its enemy, supported the theory that
the native right was paramount to such an extensive patent.
Titles from the natives were produced and were strongly
upheld, and it is said by Sullivan that what was not taken
from Gorges' patent by other means, was generally swal-
lowed up by Indian deeds.[5]

---

[1] Graham, Col. Hist., I. 183.
[2] Land Titles, 36.
[3] See p. 15, *post et seq.*
[4] Sullivan's Land Titles, 42.
[5] *Ibid.* 43.

Eventually, in 1677, the province was sold by the grandson of Gorges to Lieutenant-Governor Usher for the use of the Colony of Massachusetts Bay.[1]

" *The Incorporation of Providence Plantations, in the Narraganset Bay in New England,*" received its charter from the Parliamentary Government of England in 1644. Its charter from the King was granted in 1663.[2] The grant of lands covered substantially the territory of the present State of Rhode Island, which had already been occupied by settlers under a government established by themselves.

" *The Governor and Company of the English Colony of Connecticut, in New England in America,*" were incorporated by royal charter in 1662.[3] The territory granted comprised what is now the State of Connecticut, and also a part of New York. Parts of it were already in the hands of settlers belonging to the Connecticut and other plantations.

The royal province of New Hampshire was constituted in 1680, the chief justices in England having decided that the title and jurisdiction were in the Crown, subject, however, to the vested rights of John Mason in the soil—a reservation which rendered land titles in that province for many years uncertain.[4] The territory subsequently reverted to the jurisdiction of Massachusetts for a short time, but from 1692 it remained a separate province.[5] It included, as was claimed, the territory now known as Vermont. Grants both to individuals and towns were made by the governments successively in power.

The country called *Sagadahock,* lying between the Penobscot and the St. Croix, the possession of which had been long contested by the English and French, was, by the charter of 1692, placed under the jurisdiction of Massachusetts, and

---

[1] Willis, Hist. of Portland, 239, and Hutchinson.
[2] Arnold, History of R. I., I. 114, 284.
[3] Trumbull, Hist. of Conn., I. 259.
[4] See documents printed in Belknap's Hist. of N. H., I. Appendix.
[5] Graham, Col. Hist., I. 244–5.

that province had authority to grant the lands. But if the King did not consent to a grant within two years after it was made, it became void. By the same charter the Province of Maine (lying between the Piscataqua and Sagadahock) was incorporated with the Province of Massachusetts Bay.[1]

The rights to land conveyed by these royal grants were in all cases substantially the same. The tenure was, as of the manor of East Greenwich, in free and common socage, and not *in capite* or by knight service ; the conditions, fealty, and the payment for rent of one-fifth part of the gold and silver ore.

The effect of the provisions relating to tenure has been generally, and in some cases strangely, misunderstood. But to discuss the subject fully here would require too much space. It must suffice to say that the tenure was not more favorable than, and not different from, that established by grants of lands in England of that period, and even of much earlier date.[2] The words " as of the manor of East Greenwich" were used, not with reference to the customs of that manor, or of the County of Kent (gavelkind, etc.), but simply to negative the otherwise necessary inference that the grant was to be held *in capite*, or, to speak more accurately, *ut de corona*,[3] which would have carried with it some disadvantages under the feudal law. The words " not *in capite* " add nothing to the substance. The tenure, however, was undoubtedly as favorable to the grantees as it could well be made.

---

[1] Sullivan, Land Titles, 45, 55 ; Maine Hist. Coll., I. 239.

[2] I have met with several grants of the kind made by Queen Elizabeth, one as early as 1560. Madox, Hist. of the Exchequer, I. 621. History of Surrey, M. & B., I. 356, 357.

[3] Lowe's Case, Bacon's Works, IV. 238, etc.

III.

GRANTS OF THE COUNCIL FOR NEW ENGLAND.

The title to land in New England is traced through the Great Council for New England, which in 1620 became seized of the whole territory, and at the time of surrendering its charter, in 1635, had already granted a great part of its lands, and taken steps for a division of the remainder among its leading members.[1] But the division was not perfected, and the ungranted lands again came into the possession of the Crown.

The confused and careless way in which the grants of the council were made has been already spoken of. The subject is exceedingly complicated, and entire accuracy could only be attained, if at all, by a long and tedious investigation. But for the present purpose, fortunately, such accuracy is not necessary, as only a few of these grants are of importance either in tracing the title or illustrating the tenure of lands.

Disregarding the grants that were forfeited or abandoned, those which failed to obtain judicial support, those which were substantially confirmations of previous grants, or which covered too little territory to be described here, we find six grants which deserve particular mention. These are:

1. In 1621, a grant to John Pierce, said to have been for the benefit of the Pilgrim colonists.[2] This was rather in the nature of an agreement to convey than an actual grant of definite territory.[3]

2. In 1628, a grant to Sir Henry Roswell and others of the territory afterward known as that of Massachusetts Bay, which will be more fully described elsewhere.[4] This grant

---

[1] Lowe's Case, Bacon's Works, IV. 238, etc.

[2] This is the common theory. But the language of the charter, and of a deposition by Samuel Welles, published in Maine Hist. Soc. Coll., I. 38, make it doubtful, and tend to show that the settlement under it was on the coast of Maine.

[3] Haven, Grants under the Great Council, etc.

[4] Sullivan, Land Titles, 48.

was followed two months later by a royal charter confirming it and granting powers of government.[1]   Under an interpretation afterward held incorrect, parts of New Hampshire and Maine were comprised within its limits.

3. In 1628, a grant to William Bradford and his associates of territory intended for a fishery of the Colony of New Plymouth, extending fifteen miles on each side of the Kennebec, and up the river to Cobbiseecontee.[2]   This tract was conveyed to the freemen of the colony in 1640, and by them in 1661 sold to Tyng and others for £500.   It was afterward known as the " Kennebec Purchase."[3]

4. In 1629–30, a grant to Wm. Bradford and his associates of the territory afterward known as that of the Colony of New Plymouth ; and also of the territory on the Kennebec, already granted in 1628.[4]

5. In 1630, a grant to Beauchamp and others, called the Muscougus grant, of a territory thirty miles square on Penobscot Bay and River.   This was afterward known as the " Waldo Patent," and is still held by the heirs or assigns of the grantees.[5]

6. In 1632, a grant to R. Aldworth and G. Elbridge of the Pemaquid tract of 12,000 acres, and 100 more for every person transported within seven years.   This is still held under title from their assigns.[6]

In 1629, a large tract was granted to John Mason between the Merrimac and the Piscataqua, afterward known as New Hampshire.   A tract called Mariana, extending from the Naumkeag River (Salem) to the Merrimac, had been previously granted to him.[7]   Lands throughout this territory were

---

[1] Mass. Rec., I. 3, etc.

[2] Gardiner, Hist. of Kennebec Purchase, in Maine Hist. Coll., II. 275, etc.

[3] Gardiner, Hist. of Kennebec Purchase, in Maine Hist. Coll., II. 276. Sullivan, Land Titles, 40 (where the latter date is given 1655).

[4] Plymouth Col. Rec.

[5] Sullivan, Land Titles, 44.

[6] *Ibid.*

[7] Belknap, Hist. of N. H., III. App.

settled and granted without regard to Mason's asserted rights; but the controversies about them played a great part in the political and social history of the colonies for a long time. These controversies were not settled until 1746, when Mason's representative finally conveyed his remaining rights to twelve persons, sometimes spoken of as the Masonian proprietors. The proprietors quit-claimed on easy terms to settlers, and made grants for towns without claiming any quit-rent, and often without fees.[1] Mason's heirs, through one Allen, made claims as late as 1790, but the matter was practically disposed of long before that time.[2]

A few other grants have been sustained, but they do not seem to have affected the prevailing systems of tenure. This, indeed, is true also of some of the grants enumerated above; but they have been noticed here merely as the sources of title to extensive tracts.

The lands in New England which had not been alienated at the time of the surrender of the company's rights in 1635, are included in grants of the Crown already mentioned.[3]

IV.

COLONIAL GRANTS.

GENERAL PROVISIONS.

The territory under the jurisdiction of Massachusetts Bay included not only the original grant to the company, but also, during the more important part of their history, the territories of Maine, under its various names, and of Plymouth. The colony also claimed for a time the southern part of New Hampshire, and exercised powers of government there. It made itself felt for a long time in Rhode Island, and gave to the emigrants of Connecticut their first authority

---

[1] Belknap. II. 205.
[2] *Ibid.* III. 14; N. H. Rep. 31.
[3] See page 13, *ante.*

to form a settlement. Nor was this all. Owing to the ample privileges of the charter, the intelligence and the prosperity of the people, its land system was developed more fully, and at an earlier date, than those of the other colonies. Superior numbers, wealth and power secured for its legislation and established usages in this, as in other matters, a marked influence upon the law and customs of all New England, so that the land systems of the other colonies, as they were successively developed, took substantially the form of that of Massachusetts Bay.

In addition to all this, it must be remembered that a great part of New England was settled directly by emigrants from the Bay, and in other cases the planters were men who had at least remained long enough in that colony to become acquainted with its institutions, and to learn to look upon them as natural and necessary under the new and strange conditions of the country.

For our purpose, therefore, a careful examination of Massachusetts laws and customs is by far the most important and useful; while in regard to other colonies it will be necessary to notice only those points in which their systems differ from that which may properly be considered the typical system of New England.

Following this line of inquiry with sufficient care, we may hope to gain a clear idea of the body of rules relating to land which prevailed in this part of our country, guiding its settlement, and deeply influencing its civilization.

Orders of the Company in England.

On the 5th of March, 1629, a committee was appointed to consider a method of dividing lands so as to " avoid all contention twixt the adventurers." The subject was debated by the company a few days afterward, and referred to a new committee.[1] The plan finally adopted was as follows :[2]

Mass. Rec., I. 30, 34.

[2] *Ibid*. I. 42, 43, 44, 363.

1. Each adventurer (or shareholder) of £50 in the common stock was to have two hundred acres, and holders of other amounts in the same proportion.

2. Every adventurer might, personally, or by his servant, request the Government to allot him land. If this was not done within ten days, he might occupy any land not already improved, not exceeding one-half of his share.

3. But if the town plat was made, and known publicly, no one was to build elsewhere (except in Massachusetts Bay, under direction). And if his lot in the town plat was not assigned him within ten days after application, he might build anywhere within the plat, and improve half an acre for each £50 of stock, unless otherwise directed as to quantity by the Government.

4. Adventurers who went, or sent others at their own charge, were to have fifty acres for each person transported. Persons other than adventurers going at their own charge, with families, were to have fifty acres for the master of the family, and such further portion, " according to their charge and quality," as the Governor and council might determine, unless otherwise agreed.

5. Conveyances under seal were to be made by the company to such as desired it.

6. If a settler disliked a place taken by him under Section 2, he might choose within the allotment whenever dividend was made.[1]

In the case of colonists who were not adventurers in the common stock, the company held it fit that " they should hold and inherit their lands by services to be done on certain days in the year," as a good means "to enjoy their lands from being held *in capite*, and to support the plantation in general and in particular."[2]

---

[1] The dividend here referred to may indicate an intended general distribution by lot to all the adventurers. See letter to Endicott in 1629, Mass. Rec., I. 391.

[2] Letter to Endicott, May 28, 1629, Mass. Rec., I. 405.

There was a reason for making a distinction between the adventurers and others, for the common stock bore at first all the public charges, fortifications, support of the ministry, etc. This form of tenure, however, does not seem to have been established.[1]

Up to this point the regulations might have been those of any trading company, made with a view to the careful management of the common property. But the request made in a letter to Endicott, the company's agent in America, that he would "accommodate such as wish to have their lands together," shows already some consideration of the social needs of the settlers.[2]

Another order was made for the benefit of the stockholders when, owing to losses, it became necessary to reduce the amount of the joint stock by two-thirds; it was then agreed that the old adventurers should have in compensation " a double portion of land, according to the first portion of two hundred acres, for £50."[3] Later, when an increase of stock was needed for general purposes of the colony, it was ordered that land should be allotted at the same rate, according to the sums subscribed.[4]

Whether intended or not, the result was that grants under these provisions could not well in any case be large enough to form great estates and so interfere with the natural growth of settlements. There was no temptation as yet to hold lands with a view to an advance in price; no way of making a grant profitable, except by "improving " the lands granted. And it was long before this ceased to be true.

The restrictions as to the place of settlement were wise precautions against such a state of things as gave so much trouble to the Dutch of New Netherland, where, for a time, this point was neglected.

---

[1] Young, Chronicles of Mass. Bay, 187.
[2] Mass. Rec., I. 399.
[3] *Ibid.* 64.
[4] *Ibid.* 68.

ORDERS AFTER THE COMING OF WINTHROP.

It is quite possible that up to the time of the transfer of the company to America, a division of the land was contemplated which would have entirely frustrated the purpose of these judicious rules, and perhaps have caused the failure of the whole enterprise.[1] But, fortunately, the rules had been for some time in force when Winthrop came to the Bay, and the wisdom of their spirit had already become evident to those engaged in the establishment of the new State. The general division was not made, and the rules were observed by the new Government. Before the transfer of the company to Massachusetts Bay in 1630, grants were probably made by the company's representative in America in accordance with his instructions,[2] but afterward all grants were made by the General Court, and were generally made upon petition.[3]

At first, all islands were reserved and appropriated to the public benefit, to be let and disposed of by the Governor and assistants,[4] and, accordingly, many leases of islands were made, both to towns and individuals.[5] But at a later day they were granted like other lands. All swamps containing about one hundred acres were to lie in common.[6] But with these exceptions all lands were available for grants, either to plantations or individuals.

The estate granted was generally a fee without reservation. But in a very few cases grants were made for life, or other term, and upon payment of rent.[7]

Before making a grant, the court appointed a committee to view the desired land and report as to its suitableness.[8] The

---

[1] Mass. Rec., I. 391.
[2] *Ibid.* 391, 405.
[3] *Ibid. passim.*
[4] *Ibid.* I. 89.
[5] *Ibid.* 94, 104, 115, etc.
[6] *Ibid.* I. 111.
[7] As in the case of some of the islands just mentioned.
[8] Mass. Rec. ; Conn. Rec. *passim;* but not when the grant was to an individual. Yet see Conn. Rec., I. 359.

order for a grant sometimes gave the intended boundaries,[1] but it usually only indicated the locality, and but rarely (except when made to an individual) mentioned the quantity of land.[2]

The order for a grant sometimes named a committee to lay it out,[3] otherwise such a committee was subsequently appointed at the request of the grantee.[4] The latter course was more usual, and the committee, after "laying out" the grant, submitted their report to the court, whose confirmation of it was essential.[5] But committees did not always do their duty. In 1634, it was found necessary to appoint a general committee to set out the bounds of towns not yet set out, or in dispute;[6] and in the grant made for Sudbury, in 1656, it was provided that the grant should be void if the committee named did not make return to the next court of election.[7]

Care, too, was taken that the bounds thus granted should be well surveyed, and the lines preserved. In 1641, it was ordered that every town should set out its bounds within a twelvemonth after they were granted;[8] and in a case of gross neglect by a town, the court upheld the title of one who had in good faith laid out a farm within the limits of the grant.[9]

The committees were expected to take cognizance of the usual provision that the land should not be laid out " to the prejudice of other grants "; and in grants to individuals, the description was often " where he may find it without prejudice

[1] As in Endicott's and Cradock's. Mass. Rec., I. 97, 141.
[2] Mass. Rec.; Conn. Rec.
[3] Dummer's grant, Mass. Rec., I. 141.
[4] As in Endicott's; *ibid.* II. 259.
[5] *Ibid. passim.*
[6] *Ibid.* I. 125.
[7] *Ibid.* IV. 264.
[8] *Ibid.* I. 319. In 1647, towns were also required to perambulate their bounds every three years. Mass. Rec., II. 210. In Connecticut it was to be done every year. Conn. Rec., I. 513.
[9] Mass. Rec., IV. 368.

to any plantation, made or to be made."[1] Yet it will be noticed that grantees had but a very limited range of choice, and that grants were for some time confined to the immediate vicinity of Massachusetts Bay. And when settlements were authorized beyond Cape Ann on the eastern coast, it was probably with a definite purpose of anticipating the threatened movements of the French in that quarter ; perhaps, also, of Englishmen, who were strangers to the undertaking of the Bay colonists.[2]

All these provisions relating to land grants sufficiently indicate the watchful care that was exercised by the Government. The purpose, evidently, was not to make individual settlers rich in lands, nor even simply to dispose of land to those who would actually occupy and cultivate it all. But the resources of the company were to be used in building up a compact State of freeholders, covering a territory ample for the requirements of comfortable living, and nothing more. No inducement, no excuse, was to be given for a loose, an isolated mode of settlement, which would have enfeebled the political development of the colony, and left it at the mercy of its enemies, or, at best, dependent upon the protection of England for its very existence.

V.

COLONIAL GRANTS—(Continued).

Grants to Private Persons.

Although the leading provisions relating to this subject have already been given as applying to all grants of public lands, the grants made to individual settlers during the first period of the colony's existence merit attentive examination. We will first consider the *extent* of grants, as a thing deeply affecting the whole question of land tenure.

---

[1] Mass. Rec. *passim.* The Johnson grant was exceptional : III. 189.
[2] Winthrop, New England Hist., I. 99.

The first grant to a private person appearing in the records of Massachusetts Bay is one of 600 acres to Winthrop, in 1631, and it is the only entry for that year. In 1632, there were six grants, averaging 148 acres each; in 1633, one grant only of 50 acres. In 1634, the number rose to nine, including one of 1,000 acres to Haynes. The average, however, was only 383 acres. A large tract was granted in 1635 to Cradock (formerly Governor), extending "a mile from the riverside in all places"; and there were two other grants of 500 acres each, besides that of Taylor's Island. In 1636, there was a grant of 1,000 acres to Saltonstall. In 1637, Dudley received 1,000 acres, and there were two or three small grants besides. In 1638, there were fourteen grants, including one of 1,500 acres, which brought the average up to 372 acres for the year.

At this time a committee was appointed to report on all applications for lands, and in 1639 there were twenty-three grants, averaging 360 acres each. But after this time the number of grants is much smaller. The wants of the leading men had been provided for, and all others were referred to the towns. Thus in 1640 there were but five grants, and the same number in 1641. In 1642 and 1643, there were three each; in 1644, one; in 1645, two; in 1646 and 1647, none. But in 1648 there were five—three of them, however, in the Pequot country—in 1649, again five; and in 1650 there were two large grants. One of these was to the executors of Isaac Johnson, 3,200 acres, in consideration of his large "adventure in the stock." The other, of 3,000 acres, to Saltonstall, was in lieu of a former grant. In 1651, 1652 and 1653, there were three grants each year; in 1655 there was but one; in 1656 there were six. Thus, during a period of twenty-five years, there were little more than one hundred grants, the largest being those to Isaac Johnson's representatives (3,200 acres), Mr. Nowell's (2,000 acres),[1] Mr. Salton-

---

[1] Even this was ordered to be laid out "in two or three farms." Mass. Rec., IV. 282.

stall's (3,200 acres in all), Mrs. Winthrop's (3,000 acres),[1] and Governor Cradock's tract. John Winthrop received 3,000 acres in the Pequot country. Very few of the others received above 500 acres, and most of the grants were not more than one-half so large as that.[2]

It will be noticed that these grants were made to the men most prominent in the history of the company and of the colony —many of them magistrates and clergymen. In many cases they are expressly said to be in consideration of the "adventure" of the grantees or their ancestors, and we may safely assume that most of them were so.

But after the first few years we find a new class of grants, made in consideration of services rendered to the colony, moneys disbursed for it,[3] or else in encouragement of undertakings likely to be beneficial to it. So, at a very early date, we find that the grant to Mr. Eaton, a teacher, is on condition that "he continue his employment with us for life."[4] E. Rawson's is on condition that "he go on in the business of powder."[5] In 1641, Stephen Day received a grant, "being the first that set upon printing."[6] Goodman Stowe's, in 1642, was "for writing the laws."[7] A large grant was made in 1645 to the owners of iron works for mining;[8] and in 1648, one was made to J. Winthrop, Jr., on condition of his establishing salt works on Massachusetts Bay.[9] In 1651,

---

[1] This was made at a time when large voluntary contributions were made by towns and individuals to relieve the Governor's financial embarrassment, caused by the unfaithfulness of his bailiff. Winthrop, N. E. Hist., II. 3, Savage's note.

[2] The statements in regard to the grants of each year are made from a careful examination of the colonial records for the whole period, and are believed to be accurate.

[3] Mass. Rec., III. 413.

[4] *Ibid.* I. 262.

[5] *Ibid.* I. 263.

[6] *Ibid.* I. 344.

[7] *Ibid.* II. 14.

[8] *Ibid.* II. 125.

[9] *Ibid.* II. 243 ; Conn. Rec., I. 410.

Governor Endicott received one, on condition that he set up copper works.[1] Others received large grants for services in arranging the relations of settlers to the eastward,[2] and in the Pequot War,[3] etc. Of these was Mr. Nowell's grant, already mentioned; and there were a number of grants of this class, from 300 acres to 500 acres, given for ordinary civil services of different persons.

For some grants no cause or consideration is assigned, but it is fair to assume that these, like others, were either for services rendered, or, in the earliest years of the colony, for shares in the "adventure."

In the particulars mentioned, the early land systems of the other colonies were in substantial agreement with that of Massachusetts, except that in some (e. g., in Connecticut) there was greater freedom in regard to place of settlement. In the territory now known as Maine, the large grants from the Crown, and from the council at Plymouth, made an apparent exception to the rule of small holdings which prevailed elsewhere. Yet these large estates were not the result of the institutions of the country, but, on the contrary, were looked upon with disfavor by the people of the colonies, and with difficulty maintained among them. The transplanted feudalism of Gorges found no nourishment in the alien atmosphere of his own settlements, and many grantees would gladly have seen the breaking up of their estates. But the scarcity of settlers, and the confused state of titles, prevented the sale of lands. The great grants of Maine were doubtless an injury to the province, and hindered its development, but they have probably had no other effect upon the prevailing land system than to obstruct its natural working in the territory covered by them, which was in consequence to a great extent left waste.

A careful husbanding of vast agricultural and other resources

---

[1] Mass. Rec., III. 256.
[2] *Ibid.* III. 339.
[3] Conn. Rec., I. 70, 208, 408.

in the interest of the whole commonwealth; a methodical occupation of its territory, involving great restraint upon the individual wills of settlers, with a view to the greatest safety and prosperity of all; an avoidance of even the beginnings of great accumulations of landed property, are the clearly marked features of the early system of grants to private persons, and the same things will again appear in examining the history of grants to communities.

VI.

COLONIAL GRANTS—(Continued).

Grants to Communities.

It has been shown that, during the earlier years of the colonies, grants to individuals were small in number and in extent, and were made either on the ground of interest in the stock of the company, or of services rendered to it. But by far the greater part of the land disposed of was granted to communities of settlers, who were sometimes members of some existing community, sometimes men who had never lived in the country, grouped together from various causes. The formation and development of these communities constitute one of the most important chapters in the history of the political and social institutions of New England.

To what extent the formation of land communities in the colonies was connected with the existence of similar institutions in ancient times in England and on the Continent, is an interesting question. The studies of Maine, Maurer, Nasse and Laveleye, have shown that the village community is probably a primitive Aryan institution, and the researches of Nasse especially have shown how much of it has survived in English law and in English life. It is possible that at the beginning of the seventeenth century some features of the earlier land system no longer in actual existence were yet known to the people of the west of England, by tradition or otherwise, and certainly some traces of the ancient system were familiar to all even then.[1]

Old habits of thought survived, too, in the customs of the manor and the burgh, and especially in the parish; and, doubtless, similar economical conditions tended to produce similar social institutions.

It is not possible to adequately consider the subject in this place, nor, indeed, has it as yet been sufficiently investigated. But the resemblance between the land communities of New England and those of the Old World is certainly too striking to be overlooked.

" In the true village community," says Maine, " the village itself is an assemblage of houses, contained, indeed, within narrow limits, but composed of separate dwellings, each jealously guarded from the intrusion of a neighbor. The village lands are no longer the collective property of the community; the arable lands have been divided between the various households; the pasture lands have been partially divided; only the waste remains in common."[2] This would be recognized, by any one acquainted with the early history of our towns, as a very good description of them. Some other remarkable correspondences will be noticed in the course of this essay; but whatever may be thought of their importance, the consciously provisional nature of the land community in this country must not be lost sight of.

The immediate cause of the formation of these communities is more easily discovered. When men came in ship-loads from the mother country, large grants of land were called for, and those who had been neighbors in England naturally wished to be together in their new homes.[3] Emigrants from

---

[1] Nasse, über die Mittelälterliche Feld-gemeinschaft in England, and see evidence cited by Maine in his " Village Communities."

[2] Early History of Institutions, 81.

[3] Mass. Rec., I. 399. The Dorchester church was formed in England. Weymouth people came from England with their minister. Winthrop, N. E., I. 163.

the older settlements, too, were often kept together in a body
from the same fact of former neighborhood, and often formed
a genuine colony of some older plantation.[1] The importance
of local church relations, and the need of mutual protection,
were always strongly felt, and the sentiments of the whole
body of colonists favored the settlement of the country by
" plantations."

Efficient measures were taken to secure good organization
and good management at the outset. In the oldest settlements
the leading members of the Government were leaders also in
their respective towns, and general legislation for a time was
not needed. But the principles of the founders of the colonies
required that new plantations should be managed in strict
subordination to the interests of the whole, and this they
accomplished by the aid of various provisions connected with
the grants.

To this end, in addition to the measures already mentioned,
committees were named to take charge of the allotment of
lands and the admission of inhabitants, thus insuring conformity to the policy of the Government. So, in 1634,
Winthrop, Humphrey and Endicott were ordered " to divide
the lands at Ipswich to particular persons as in equity they
shall think meet."[2] When the settlement of Hampton was
authorized, it was ordered that nothing should be done without allowance of a commission consisting of Messrs. Bradstreet,
Winthrop, Jr., and Rawson.[3] The same thing was done in
the cases of Sudbury,[4] Nashaway[5] and other plantations,[6] and
it became the general practice. That it was not always done,
may be due to the fact that the court was careful not to
authorize new plantations unless they were to be in a measure

---

[1] Thus Winslow was a Dorchester colony ; Woodstock was settled by
men from Roxbury, etc.

[2] Mass. Rec., I. 136.

[3] *Ibid.* 236.

[4] *Ibid.* I. 271.

[5] Mass. Rec., II. 136.

[6] Sometimes in Conn.; see Conn. Rec., I. 414 ; 71, etc.

under the influence of men in whom confidence could be placed, and commonly acted upon their application. When such leadership of the undertaking was secured, the court was ready to give its sanction and its aid.

The earliest settlements in Massachusetts Bay had, so far as appears in the records, no formal authorization. They were so near to each other that all questions could be disposed of by common agreement or the word of the magistrate; but they soon crystallized into a number of separate communities.

In 1633, reports that the French were attempting the colonization of the coast to the eastward excited apprehension, and it was decided that a plantation should be begun at Agawam (Ipswich), " lest an enemy, finding it void, should possess and take it from us."[1] Two months later, John Winthrop, Jr., with twelve others, went there to begin the settlement,[2] and the General Court then ordered that no others should go there without its leave.[3] The next year a committee of the court was authorized to allot lands within four miles of the village.[4] This was the first plantation in New England made under the auspices of any colonial authority.

A year later (1634) the pressure for land began to be felt at the Bay, and the colonization of the interior and the remoter seacoast began—a movement which, although stronger at some times than at others, was thenceforth practically continuous.

The inhabitants of Newtown (Cambridge) were the first to complain for the want of land, and, obtaining leave of the court to seek some convenient place, they sent men to Agawam and Merrimack to report.[5] Some also went to visit the

---

[1] Winthrop, N. E., I. 99.
[2] *Ibid.* 101.
[3] Mass. Rec., I. 103.
[4] See *ante*, 29.
[5] Mass. Rec., I. 119 ; Winthrop, I. 132.

Connecticut River, and at the next court they asked leave to remove thither.   The subject was long and earnestly debated, but the adverse vote of the assistants for the time prevented the giving of the desired authority.[1]

The next year some of the leading men of Ipswich were allowed to form a plantation at Newbury,[2] and a company of twenty-one families from England, with their minister, was authorized to form a plantation at Weymouth, where there was already a small settlement.[3]

The state of affairs in England was rapidly growing worse, and immigration to this country was in consequence greatly increased.   Grants were made for plantations at several places, not far from existing settlements.   But the time had come for the occupation of more distant points, and preparations were made for emigration on a large scale from the plantations of the coast.

In urging their request for permission to remove, the petitioners had set forth the fruitfulness and commodiousness of the region, and the danger of leaving it to be possessed by others, Dutch or English.[4]   The latter was a strategic reason, which doubtless had its weight (as in the course of the settlement of Ipswich).[5]   But the principal attraction was, without doubt, the prospect of abundant provision for cattle in the great meadows of the central valley.   The colonists had much live stock.   Wood says, in 1634, that they had " 1,500 head of cattle, besides 4,000 goats, and swine innumerable."[6] Lechford also speaks of the " good store of cattle,"[7] and it appears that the transportation of cattle, horses, etc., with Winthrop cost £12,000.[8]   The neat cattle carried to New

---

[1] Winthrop, I. 140.
[2] *Ibid.* I. 160 ; Mass. Rec., I. 146.
[3] *Ibid.* I. 163.
[4] *Ibid.* 140.
[5] *Ante* 30.
[6] New England's Prospect, 54.
[7] Plaine Dealing.
[8] Josselyn, Two Voyages to New England, 132.

Plymouth in 1624 throve and increased exceedingly,[1] and in 1642 there were already 1,000 sheep.[2] It is evident, therefore, that live stock was very abundant, and in our climate a supply of hay as well as pasturage is so essential that Wood, in describing towns, always mentions that they " have hay-ground " ; but we know now that his accounts of unlimited sources of supply were exaggerated. We cannot be surprised, therefore, to find that the course of settlement follows the line of wide alluvial valleys, especially those of the Connecticut and its tributaries. Rich meadows were the main object of the emigrant's desires, and this accounts for the order of settlement of different places. It explains, too, why the orders for grants frequently directed[3] (and seem always to have implied) that the tract granted was to comprise both upland (including timber) and meadow, thus supplying all the wants of the community. This practice was followed by the plantations in allotting lands and regulating their use.

The extent of grants made to communities is a point of interest, both because the lands thus came into the hands of a definite number of persons, and were also for the most part soon divided among them, and also because of the political subdivisions which were based upon them.

As to the extent of grants, we have seen that at Ipswich the lands were to extend four miles from the town. There were other cases where tracts of eight miles square were granted—*e. g.*, Groton,[4] Mendon,[5] and the grant on the Saco River for Newbury[6]—and a ten miles' square was offered to Captain Hawthorne and others proposing to make a settlement forty or fifty miles west of Springfield. On the other

[1] Josselyn, Two Voyages to New England, 146.
[2] New England's First Fruits, 39. Winthrop, I. 160.   The Dorchester colonists lost near £2,000 worth of cattle the first winter in Conn. Winthrop, I. 184.
[3] Mass. Rec., I. 156.
[4] *Ibid.* III. 388.
[5] *Ibid.* IV. 445.
[6] *Ibid.* 402.

hand, some of the oldest towns were quite small; but in general a tract six miles square, or its equivalent, was thought of the best size for a plantation. As to its relation to the number of planters, we find, in the case of Groton, that a committee of the General Court thought that the tract was large enough for sixty families, which would have given them over one square mile each.[1] But the report of the same committee shows that this was not looked upon as the permanent limit of population, and we are told by Winthrop that "a principal motive which led the court to grant * * such vast bounds was that when the towns should be increased by their children and servants growing up, etc., they might have place to erect villages where they might be planted, and so the land improved to the more common benefit."[2]

Many villages grew up within the limits of the older plantations, and eventually became separate towns. Thus Charlestown originally (until 1641) included what afterward became the towns of Malden, Stoneham, Woburn, Burlington, Somerville, West Cambridge, Medford, and part of Cambridge.[3] Many plantations received additional grants for the express purpose of enabling them to form new villages. Thus, in 1639, land was granted to Salem for a new village[4] (afterward Wenham), and the next year Shawshin (Billerica) was granted to Cambridge for the same purpose.[5] Dedham also received additions which became Wrentham and Medfield.[6] And so in other places. In 1683, a tract in the interior eight miles square was granted to Roxbury, which when settled received the name of Woodstock (Conn.).[7] The granting to towns of tracts at a distance for settlement subsequently became a common practice. The settling of a

[1] Mass. Rec., IV. 9.
[2] Winthrop, N. E., II. 254.
[3] Brook's Hist. of Medford, 2.
[4] Mass. Rec., I. 279. -
[5] *Ibid.* 330.
[6] Annals of Dedham.
[7] Ellis's Hist. of Roxbury, 72.

new plantation was a very important matter, and was formally resolved upon and prepared for by the mother town. The Scituate people who settled Barnstable, when expecting to go to Sippecan, "prayed for direction in electing committees for setting down the township."[1] The land was sometimes sold by the proprietors in the old town to the settlers. Thus, Dedham in 1661, in voting to settle what was afterward Wrentham, grants six hundred acres to the settlers, and afterward gives up all claim to them, for which they are to pay £160, in instalments.[2] Roxbury, in settling Woodstock, voted that if thirty men should go they should have one-half of it, in one square, at their selection, and £500 to assist them, to be laid out in public buildings. The other inhabitants were to have the rest.[3]

It was important that when a tract of land was granted, either to an individual or for a new plantation, it should be speedily occupied, as the making of still other grants might depend upon it. But it would seem that some neglected to improve their grants, for in 1634 it was ordered that if any large grant was not improved within three years, the court might dispose of it.[4] In the case of plantations, it was generally made a condition that a certain number of families (commonly twenty) should be settled within a given time (usually from one to three years), so that a ministry might be supported. Sometimes, also, it was stipulated that settlement should begin within a certain time.[5]

It was necessary that unfriendly settlers should be excluded from the new plantations, and also that existing settlements should not be unnecessarily weakened. So it was ordered, in 1635, that none should go to the new plantation

---

[1] Letter of Rev. Mr. Lothrop, in Freeman, Cape Cod, II. 275.

[2] Annals of Dedham.

[3] Ellis's Roxbury, *loc. cit.*

[4] Mass. Rec., I. 114. Mr. Dudley, however, had a grant of 1,000 acres, "without limit to time of improvement." *Ibid.* 206.

[5] Mass. Rec., Conn. Rec.

at Marblehead without leave of court or of two magistrates;[1] and the following year the same powers were conferred upon the majority of the magistrates with reference to all new plantations.[2]

But the Government went further, and aided the settlement of new plantations more actively, and, when important to the colony, by extraordinary acts and measures. So, when settlement was authorized at Newbury, an advance post, it was resolved that the court should have power to see that it received a sufficient number to make a town.[3]

Again, when Concord was settled, the magistrates were authorized to impress carts, etc., for those who had goods to be carried thither;[4] and at Hampton men were so impressed to build a house forthwith.[5]

The new plantations were exempted from the payment of public charges for a variable number of years up to six or even more, in the more remote and hazardous situations.[6]

The interests of individuals were often made subordinate to those of plantations, as those were to the colonies.[7] A house built without leave from the town, if prejudicial, might be demolished and the persons removed.[8] Private lands might be taken for the purposes of the settlement, but the rights of grantees were protected, and provision was made for compensation in case of damage.[9]

---

[1] Mass. Rec., I. 147.
[2] *Ibid.* I. 167.   A settlement at Hampton was first authorized.
[3] *Ibid.* 146.
[4] *Ibid.* 157, 182.
[5] *Ibid.* 167.
[6] *Ibid. passim.*   Saco River Settlement, IV. 424.
[7] *Ibid.* I. 147 ; II. 48.
[8] *Ibid.* I. 168.
[9] *Ibid.* I. 68, 147.

VII.

LAND COMMUNITIES.

Commoners and Non-Commoners.

The last stage in the process of distribution is that in which lands pass from the community to its individual members, involving the dissolution of the community itself, or its transformation into a political community.

" In Swiss villages," says Laveleye, " the Beisassen, or simple residents, frequently have no share in the 'Allmends.' The Beisassen have often complained of this distinction, which has given rise to violent struggles between the reformers, who demand equal rights for all, and the conservatives, who endeavor to maintain the old exclusion. * * * Generally, arrangements have been adopted securing certain rights to the mere residents."[1] We have here, in a few words, the history of the land communities of our own colonial period, wherever the inevitable collision of hostile interests has not been prevented by some happy combination of circumstances.

The distinction between " commoners " and " non-commoners " was very early made, and these names themselves were in general use. But the term " proprietor " was also employed with the same meaning as " commoner," and soon came to be considered the proper legal term; and we find now in our towns the records of the owners of common lands always under the name of " proprietors' records." The " commoners " were originally those to whom the General Court had made a grant of land in common for settlement, very often, as we have seen, without giving the grantees entire, unfettered control. They formed, as has been held, a *quasi*-corporation, having the powers of other corporations for certain specified purposes.[2] The right of a commoner

---

[1] La Propriété Primitive, 23.
[2] 3 Verm. Rep. 553. Mass. Rep.

might be conveyed or inherited like other real estate, and one
who thus became entitled to a right was not necessarily an
inhabitant, nor was he necessarily entitled to vote in the
town-meetings, when township privileges had been conferred
upon the inhabitants of a plantation. On the other hand,
it by no means followed that because a man was entitled to
a vote in the town, he was also entitled to a voice in the
control of the common lands, or that he had any right to
them whatever. The land community and the political community were distinct bodies, capable of dealing with other
persons and bodies, and with each other as separate juristic
persons.[1]

Thus we find votes of the town according rights to the
" proprietors," or even making engagements with them.

The proprietors, too, might make grants to the town as to
any other parties, as in the case of Ipswich (Mass.), where
they granted the " cow commons," north of the river, com-
prising 3,244 acres, to the inhabitants of the town (which
probably included all the commoners), to be improved.[2] The
same proprietors, in 1788, granted to the town their whole
interest in the commons, to help pay debts incurred in the
Revolution.[3]

But, although the distinction between the two bodies is well
marked and generally observed, in practice they were sometimes blended, and the strictness with which they were at any
time kept apart depends upon a variety of circumstances.

In plantations where the inhabitants were all commoners,
or where there were few who were not such, the distinction
was commonly disregarded at first. The two bodies were

---

[1] This is the case in many Teutonic village-communities, the result of a
long course of changes in the original system. See v. Maurer, Gesch. d.
Dorfverf. II. 247, etc. Especially in Switzerland, *ibid.* p. 253. Comp.
Laveleye, *loc. cit.*

[2] Felt, Hist. of Ipswich, etc., 14.

[3] *Ibid.* 161. The tract called the Town Common was granted to the
town of Cambridge (Mass.) by the proprietors, to lie undivided, etc., forever. Proprietors' Records in Holmes's Hist. of Cambridge, 35.

substantially identical, and acted as one. At the meetings of the freemen, matters relating both to the land rights of the community and to the local government of the plantations were settled, and the same records served for the town and for the proprietors. So, for instance, in Groton, settled in 1655, there were no separate meetings of the proprietors prior to 1713.[1] But as the number of non-commoners became considerable, the original settlers multiplying, and newcomers streaming in, the commoners found it necessary to look after their rights. In the town of Hampton (N. H.), where three years after the settlement (1641) persons who were not freemen were present at the town meetings, as appears by the records, it was voted in 1662 that "no man be considered an inhabitant, or act in town affairs, * * * but he that hath one share at least of commonage, according to the first division." [2]

In 1700, it was voted that no one should vote unless a freeholder ; and " none to vote to dispose of lands, unless he is a commoner," etc.[3] Thus, by this simple contrivance, the necessity of two organizations was for a time avoided. But this was not long deemed sufficient, and separate meetings of the " proprietors " and of the town became the rule, and were held so long as any common lands remained. Separate records of these proprietors' meetings are very generally found in the older towns, where they form legal evidence of title.

In some of the towns, the need of protecting the rights of commoners was strongly felt almost from the beginning. This was especially the case in the oldest plantations, which were most directly affected by the stream of immigration from England. In Watertown (Mass.), even in 1635, it was voted, "In consideration there be too many inhabitants in the town, and the town thereby in danger to be ruinated,

---

[1] Butler, Hist. of Groton.
[2] Records of the town of Hampton.
[3] *Ibid.*

that no forrainers coming into the town, or any family arising among ourselves, shall have any benefit, either of commonage or of land undivided, but what they shall purchase, except they buy a man's right wholly in the town."[1] In 1660, it was said in Ipswich that "the common lands are over-burdened by dwelling-houses. No house henceforth erected is to have any right to commonage, or to the common lands, without express leave." And this order was confirmed by the General Court.[2]

The distinctive rights of the proprietors were in general fully acknowledged by the town. At Haverhill, in 1702, the town refused to act on a petition, "because not directed to the proprietors of lands, but to the town, many of whom have no power to vote in the disposal of lands."[3]

At Wenham, when the power of the commoners to divide lands was questioned, the town confirmed it, and granted the lands to those who had drawn them.[4] But the rights of the respective parties were not always so clearly understood, and it is certain that some had honest doubts upon the subject, and in some cases opinions prevailed which were actually wrong. It may[5] be conjectured that the readiness of the towns to recognize the rights of the commoners depended very much upon the relative strength of the commoners in the town meetings. Where the majority of the voters were commoners, although there might be discontent, and although that discontent might be loudly expressed, there would be no attempts to seize the power to control or dispose of the com-

---

[1] Bond, Hist. of Watertown, 995.
[2] Felt, Hist. of Ipswich, 16. Mass. Rec.
[3] Chase, Hist. of Haverhill, 205.
[4] Allen, Hist. of Wenham, 50.
[5] The Selectmen of Roxbury were directed, in 1692, to consult authority and obtain their judgment concerning the right proprietors of common lands. "Some claimed that they belonged to the first proprietors, and not to the body at large." Ellis, Hist. of Roxbury, 72-3. And in Barnstable there were hot debates upon the same questions. Freeman, Cape Cod, II. 202-3.

mon lands. But there is abundant evidence that where the numbers of the non-commoners were sufficient, either alone or in combination with a fraction of the commoners, there was no lack of a disposition to get control, and to exercise that control for their own advantage; and this was done sometimes with little regard to legal rights.

In the same town of Haverhill, to which I have referred as an instance of clear recognition of the proper ownership of common land, there were long-continued troubles about that very point, and the non-commoners, after making to the commoners a proposition to share with them, which was refused, tried to exercise control, and to grant lands. As the commoners proceeded to make divisions of the commons, and continued to do so, the feeling became very bitter. In 1723, committees were chosen by both parties to make some agreement, and some small grants were made to the non-commoners to quiet them. But the troubles revived and the strife grew worse. Two sets of town officers were chosen, and the General Court had to decide between them. But the proprietors prevailed, and at length the opposition was given up.[1]

But in other cases the proprietors did not fare so well. In Simsbury (Conn.), in 1719, the town, after reserving commonage, voted to sequester the rest to the town, and to grant it as the majority—not in numbers, but in ratable estate—should determine. This gave great offense, but the town made many grants. In 1723, a town-meeting was held which lasted for three successive days and nearly one whole night, and grants were made to the greater part of the inhabitants.

The proprietors appealed to the Legislature, but got no relief until the general law was passed some years later. After that they managed exclusively what lands were left, but it does not appear that they ever received any redress for the injuries inflicted by the action of the town.

---

[1] Chase, Hist. of Haverhill.

In the nature of things, there must have been contentions about these questions very generally in the towns of New England, although under some circumstances they were long postponed.[1] In the towns of the Connecticut Valley the subject of dividing the commons was not much agitated until the latter part of the 17th century. But the agitation continued with intervals for half a century or more. Jonathan Edwards, in a letter written in 1751, said there had been in Northampton for forty or fifty years " two parties, somewhat like the court and country parties of England, if I may compare small things with great. The first party embraced the great proprietors of land, and the parties concerned about land and other matters." [2]   .

In some cases the differences between the two parties were settled by committees from their own number,[3] or by referees from other towns.[4]

But extreme measures and even the necessity of arbitration were commonly avoided by the good sense of both parties, and by the public spirit frequently shown by the proprietors. The reason for making grants of more territory than was needed for the immediate wants of the first settlers has already been stated,[5] and it was, in most cases, well understood. The legal title was in the original planters, but there was in most cases a moral trust in favor of later comers, and, although sometimes only under pressure, the obligation was very generally recognized—at least so long as the commons exceeded the requirements of the commoners. There were two ways of satisfying the claims of non-commoners. The first was by increasing the number of commoners, and this was not infrequently done. The old records give evidence of the custom, mentioning, without comment, the admission of com-

---

[1] Phelps, Hist. of Simsbury, 80 *et seq.*
[2] Judd. Hist. of Hadley, etc., 281. Comp. Maine, Early Hist. of Inst. 84.
[3] See p. 40, *ante.*
[4] As at Barnstable. See Freeman, Hist. of Cape Cod, II. 202.
[5] *Ante,* 33.

moners.[1] And in some cases the number of commoners varied according to a fixed system.

But more usual was the granting of certain lands to new-comers without any accompanying rights to commonage. This was done either for individuals by name, or to all of a given class. At Barnstable four acres were voted to every widow.[2] Oftener still the newcomers were included with the commoners in a general division of lands to all the inhabitants, by which, however, no right to share in further divisions was conveyed. Thus at Eastham, in 1652, a division of common lands was made " to first settlers and newcomers." [3] So, too, at Ipswich, as we have seen, a large tract was granted to the inhabitants, with the commoners, to be improved.[4] In the towns of the Connecticut Valley, and some towns of the New Haven Colony, it seems to have been usual to make such division, the rights of the original settlers being sufficiently protected by the principle of the allotment, of which we shall speak.[5]

VIII.

LAND COMMUNITIES — (CONTINUED).

DIVISION OF COMMON LANDS.

In the allotment of lands in the different towns, several things were taken into consideration. For the simplicity of the rules adopted by Wenham (Mass.), with but one dissenting voice, " that all commoners should stand equally, both

---

[1] Felt, Hist. of Ipswich, 161 ; 144 new commoners were admitted there. Records of Hampton, etc. At Duxbury, in 1710, *the young men* were granted, on petition, half a share. Town Records, in Winsor, Hist. of Duxbury.

[2] Freeman, Cape Cod, II. 379.

[3] *Ibid.*

Felt, Ipswich, 14.

[5] Lambert, Hist. of New Haven, etc. Judd, Hist. of Hadley, etc.

as to quantity and quality,"[1] had but few imitators. Numbers were, of course, an essential element in the computation,
but estate was of still more consequence and prominence, and
was very generally made the principal basis of division.
The valuation of each man's estate was for this purpose
made from the tax-list, according to the rates paid by him
toward the public expenses. Thus, at Haverhill, in 1643, it
was voted that "he that was worth £200, to have 20 acres to
his house-lot * * * and so every one under that sum to
have acres proportionable for his house-lot, together with
meadow and common, and planting ground, proportionably."[2]
At Ipswich, 1665, lands were divided among the commoners
according to rates.[3] So, too, at Dedham,[4] where a somewhat
complicated rule prevailed; in Hartford and the other Connecticut River towns;[5] in the settlements along the Sound,[6]
and in many other places.

Where the town itself did not prescribe the mode of
division, the committee having the division in charge would
commonly favor those having estate, as we see in the case of
the Boston committee, about whose election there was so
much trouble in 1634. Winthrop says: "The inhabitants
of Boston met to choose seven men who should divide the
town lands among them. In their choice they left out Mr.
Winthrop, Coddington and other of the chief men; only they
chose one of the elders and a deacon, and the rest of the
inferior sort, and Mr. Winthrop had the greater number
before one of them by a voice or two. This they did as fear-
ing that the richer men would give the poorer sort no great
proportions of land, but would rather leave a great part at
liberty for new comers and for commons, which Mr. Win-

---

[1] Allen, Hist. of Wenham, 2.
[2] Records of Haverhill, in Chase, Hist. of H. 56.
[3] Felt, Hist. of Ipswich, 16.
[4] Annals of Dedham, 82.
[5] Judd, Hist. of Hadley, etc.
[6] Lambert, Hist. of New Haven, etc.

throp had oft persuaded them to as best for the town." The elders were offended and Winthrop declined. But a new election was held, after a talk by Mr. Cotton, and Winthrop and other leading men were appointed to dispose of the lands as they should see fit. Winthrop says of their course that it "was partly to prevent the neglect of trades * * * and partly that there might be place to receive such as should come after; seeing it would be very prejudicial to the commonwealth if men should be forced to go far off for land, while others had much, and could make no use of it more than to please their eye with."[1] This account well illustrates both the spirit of the leaders, and the opposition sometimes found. But we have seen that at an early day it became the practice of the General Court to name committees to superintend the organization of new plantations, and one of their most important functions was the division of lands among the first settlers. In a few cases the Government fixed a maximum which no grant could exceed until a certain number had joined the community.[2] But the whole subject was generally left to the discretion of the committee. In this way conformity to the policy of the Government was insured.

The opposition to such a plan of division which might have been expected was prevented in great measure, partly by the evident reasonableness of the general principle that land should be given to those who could use it, and partly by the provisions made to guard against excessive inequality in the shares allotted to different persons.

At Springfield (Mass.) it was the original agreement (1636) that every inhabitant should have a convenient proportion of land for a house-lot, "as we shall see meete for every one's quality and estate." Then, further, "we shall observe this rule about dividing of planting ground and meadow, in all planting ground to regard chiefly persons who arc most apt to use such ground. And in all meadow

---

[1] Winthrop, N. E., I. 152.
[2] Mass. Rec., IV. Part II. 500; V. 22.

and pasture, to regard chiefly cattle and estate, because estate is like to be improved in cattle, and such ground is aptest for their use. *And yet we agree*, that no person that is master of a lot, though he have not cattle, shall have less than 3 acres of planting ground, &c."[1] In Northampton, allotments were to be to families, according to "names, estates and qualifications," but every single man was to have 4 acres of meadow, besides the rest of his division, and every head of a family 6 acres.[2] In the division of Hadley lands, each proprietor received allotments according to a sum annexed to his name, called estate, varying from £50 to £200, and probably the result of amicable agreement. At another time, an estate of £150 was credited to each proprietor, perhaps in addition to his "rate." In this town, although lands were divided according to each one's real estate as it stood in the tax-list, we find that the head of a family *without real estate* drew on different occasions 50, 50 and 11 acres, respectively. In one, a £50 allotment was given to every householder, and £25 for each male minor above 16.

Although in this way "the wealthy man had as much on account of his slave as the poor man on his own account," the poor man was well provided for, and we are told that, apart from the grants just mentioned, among the original proprietors of Hadley, the largest share was only four times greater than the smallest, and later five times greater; and that "the equity of divisions was never called in question."[3] In a division made at Ipswich in 1665, lands were divided according to rates in the proportion of 4, 6 and 8, thus giving the poorest one-half as much as the richest.[4] The same pro-

---

[1] Records of Springfield, in Holland, Western Mass. I. 25.

[2] *Ibid.* I. 47.

Barnstable, by general consent, divided one-third to every house-lot equally; one-third to the number of names that are immovable—*i. e.*, to such as are married or 25 years of age—and the other one-third according to men's estates. Freeman, Cape Cod, II. 256.

[3] Holland, I. 33.

[4] Felt, Hist. of Ipswich, 101.

portion was observed in some other towns, although sometimes the inequality was much greater, and the rates varied in different divisions even in the same town. The later divisions of woodland in the river towns were far more unequal than the earlier distributions of intervale.[1]

Dedham (Mass.) had some additional special rules for allotment, and among them that servants should be referred to men's estates, and according to men's estates; that allotments should be "according to men's rank, quality, desert and usefulness, either in church or commonwealth. That men of useful trades may have material to improve the same, be encouraged and have land, as near home as may be convenient, and that husbandmen that have abilities to improve more than others, be considered."[2]

In this town (Dedham) a portion of land was always reserved for town, church and school, and reservations of land for school, church and ministry were usual in the towns, even if not required by the conditions of their grant.[3]

In making a grant for a plantation near Lake Quinsigamond, the court inserted the condition that in the allotment of lands, 200 or 300 acres, with meadow, should be reserved for the commonwealth.[4] The precedent was followed in 1670 in the grant for a plantation south of Springfield and Westfield,[5] in those for Squakeage[6] and Lancaster,[7] Dunstable,[8] etc., and soon became the general practice.

In the first case cited, power was given to the committee of the court to settle tenants for lives, or for terms, paying a small rent. But nothing is usually said of such a plan in making the later reservations.[9]

---

[1] Judd, Hadley, etc., 30, 31.   [2] Annals of Dedham, 82.

[3] Annals of Dedham ; and see Freeman, Cape Cod, II. 202 (Barnstable) ; 379 (Eastham); 245 (Sandwich); and Lambert, New Haven, etc., 96, etc.

[4] Mass. Rec., IV. Part II. 409.

[5] *Ibid.* IV. Part II. 469.   [6] *Ibid.* 529.   [7] *Ibid.* 545 (1 sq. m. reserved).   [8] *Ibid.* 571.

[9] Leases of public or common lands, by colony or town, were not very common. But Duxbury seems to have leased extensively, especially meadows. Town Records, in Winsor, Hist. of Duxbury.

The case of the plantations along the Sound differed somewhat from that of other towns in New England. These did not occupy territory granted by any colonial or other government. The lands had been bought outright by the principal men, and were held in trust for the people, who, after contributing to pay expenses, drew lots in proportion to their contribution.[1]

In the New Haven Colony, it was ordered "that every planter give in the names of the heads of the persons in his family (wherein his wife, together with himself and children, only are to be reckoned), with an estimate of his estate, according to which he will both pay his proportion in all rates and public charges, * * * and expect lands in all divisions, which shall be generally made to the planters."[2] In the first division the rate was 5 acres to £100, and 2½ acres for each person.[3]

In Guilford, it was agreed that "every one should pay his proportional part or share toward all the charges and expenses for purchasing, settling, surveying and carrying on the necessary public affairs of the plantations, and that all divisions of the land should be made in exact proportion to the sums they advanced and expended." Divisions were made accordingly. But even here no one could put in more than £500 without permission of the freemen.[4]

Milford, however, "sequestered" a belt of land around the town two miles wide, and divided lands from time to time among the inhabitants according to their estate in lists of different years. The number of proprietors was, therefore, variable, rising, *c. g.*, between 1686 and 1712 from 109 to 197. But a division of 1805 was based upon the list of 1686, the earlier number having been thus fixed upon.[5]

Divisions and grants of common lands could generally be

---

[1] Dwight, Hist. of Conn. 84.
[2] New Haven Col. Rec. 192.
[3] *Ibid.*
[4] Lambert, New Haven, etc., 163.
[5] *Ibid.* 96.

made by a majority vote, and the power was often delegated to selectmen or committees. But Milford required the consent of three-fourths of the inhabitants,[1] and in Eastham (Mass.) the action of the majority was restricted by provision that the grant, to be valid, should "be subjected to the negative of men chosen for that purpose, and shall be laid out and bounded on their approval."[2]

In addition to the division of lands among the proprietors or the inhabitants, the towns, like the colonial governments, sometimes made grants to individuals, especially to those whose services were or might be valuable. Thus Groton made grants to encourage the establishment of a mill;[3] Haverhill did the same,[4] as did many other towns. Lands were also sold occasionally for various purposes, as at Barnstable in 1691 (to raise money for the expenses of obtaining the Colony Charter),[5] but this was never done to any great extent.

IX.

LAND COMMUNITIES.—(CONTINUED).

RESTRICTIONS UPON ALIENATION.

A very interesting feature in the early history of the institutions of New England is the care taken to preserve the original character of the community, and to control its membership. As the entire right of commoners might be assigned, and usually passed with a grant of land by a commoner, it was not enough for the town to retain the right of admitting freemen; it also needed to have control over sales of land made by its members, especially of house lots. This control has been very generally claimed and exercised by land com-

---

[1] Lambert, New Haven, etc., 96.
[2] Freeman, Cape Cod, II. 376.
[3] Butler, Hist. of Groton, 32.
[4] Chase, Haverhill, 84.
[5] Freeman, Cape Cod, II. 279.

munities, wherever found, and for similar reasons; and the
resemblance in this respect between the institutions of communities so widely separated in time and place is very
marked and worthy of notice.

In the village communities of Russia, a man may not sell
his house and land to one who is a stranger to the " *mir* "
without the consent of the inhabitants of the village, who have
always the right of pre-emption.[1] Similar rules prevailed in
Germany,[2] France[3] and Ireland;[4] and the right of the inhabitants of a village to reclaim land in case of sale to a stranger
is, according to Laveleye, found everywhere.[5]

The land communities of New England formed no exception to this, but the rules which were adopted in them to
effect the purpose, although similar in substance, were of
varying degrees of strictness.

In Connecticut, a law of 1659 declares that " No inhabitant shall have power to make sale of his accommodation of
house and lands until he have first propounded the sale thereof
to the town where it is situate, and they refuse to accept of the
sale tendered."[6] Elsewhere the subject was left to the towns.
The General Court of Massachusetts did, indeed, once raise
the question whether towns could restrain individuals from
sale of their lands or houses; but no action is recorded, and
the proceedings of the towns were not interfered with.[7] At
Guilford (Conn.), no one could sell or alien his share, or any
part of it, or purchase of another, unless by consent of the community.[8] Watertown (Mass.), in 1638, made a provision

---

[1] Laveleye, La Propriété Primitive, 11.

[2] Maurer, " Das weit verbreitete Vorkaufsrecht der Dorfmarkgenossen,"
u. s. w. ; see Dorfverf. I. 320.

[3] See the Coutume de Bayonne, cited by Maurer in the same, 322. " Le
voisin et habitant de la dite ville est preféré à l'etranger acheteur."

[4] Ancient Laws of Ireland, cited in Maine, Early Hist. of Institutions,
109.

[5] La Propr. Prim. 152.

[6] Conn. Rec. 1. 351.

[7] Mass. Rec. 1. 201.

[8] Lambert, New Haven, etc., 163.

"against selling town lots to forrainers,"[1] and Wenham, 1642, voted that " in case any wished to remove from the village, they were to offer their places for sale first to the plantation."[2] Barnstable ordered the same, and further, " in case the plantation buy it not, then he shall provide a purchaser whom the town shall approve, and if the town do not provide a chapman in two months, he may then sell it to whom he will."[3] Billerica allowed the proprietor of a " 10 acre privilege " to sell a " 5 acre privilege," and one who had not more than a " 10 acre privilege " could not dispose of it, even to his children, unless the town had refused to make them a grant.[4] Meadfield imposed the restriction for seven years only.[5] The need of such legislation after some years was not felt as at first, and the restrictions eventually were everywhere disregarded.

COMMON FIELDS.

The proportion of land cultivated in common varied greatly at different periods and in different places. At first, common cultivation was on a much larger scale than it was at a later day. For, the practice being adopted as a matter of necessity in most cases,[6] whenever the necessity ceased to be felt, the practice was no longer favored. They sometimes included nearly all the " improved " lands of the town, as at Simsbury (Conn.), where a committee of the General Court laid out two fields extending seven miles on each side of the river.[7] In other cases, although they did not include all the lands, they yet included some lands in which all the people of the town were interested. It was to such fields that the

---

[1] Town Records, in Bond, Hist. of Watertown, 995.

[2] Allen, Hist. of Wenham, 26.

[3] Freeman, Cape Cod, II. 254.

[4] Farmer, Hist. Memoir, 8.

[5] Annals of Dedham, 99.

[6] " Necessity constraining the improvement of much land in common." Conn. Col. Rec. I. 101.

[7] See Phelps, Simsbury, 80.

laws of Connecticut and Massachusetts referred, giving authority over them to the townsmen or selectmen of the town, or, where there were none, to the major part of the freemen,[1] to order the manner of their improvement. Massachusetts afterward put the power over common meadows and pastures in the hands of the proprietors of the greatest part,[2] as she had done at first in case of cornfields.[3] It is probable, however, that this law refers to groups of owners smaller in number than the whole body of commoners. Common fields of this sort were found in most of the towns. Sometimes they were formed from lack of the means to fence separately; sometimes from the difficulty of fencing, as on the extensive intervale-lands of the Connecticut, and often from mere considerations of convenience. In Milford (Conn.), the town lots were at first fenced in common, and soon after three large common fields were formed. Much of the land in that town was thus cultivated, and " field meetings " were held to manage the common property.[4]

Lands were even granted to be thrown together into a common field.[5] They were sometimes meadow, sometimes pasture, and sometimes plowing land.[6]

Fences were maintained by each owner according to his share in the land enclosed. Sometimes gates or bridges were thus maintained instead of a portion of fence, and in Milford and Stratford lands were held upon condition of such service,[7] the proper care of them being of importance to the whole town.

The bounds of lands lying in common were to be perambu-

---

[1] Mass. Rec. II. 49 ; Conn. Rec. I. 101, 214.

[2] *Ibid.* II. 195.

[3] *Ibid.* 39.

[4] Lambert, New Haven, etc., 96–97 (from Town Records, Lib. I. 87). See also Town Records of Stratford, Lib. I.

[5] Bond, Watertown, 995.

[6] Mass. Rec. II. 49.

[7] Milford Town Records (in Lambert, New Haven, etc., 96). Stratford Town Records.

lated by the particular proprietors, and boundary marks (mere stones) to be carefully kept up.[1]

A resemblance will be noticed between these smaller groups of cultivators in common and the alp and vineyard communities in Europe.[2]

HOME LOTS, ACRE RIGHTS, PITCHES.

Home Lots or House Lots.—The exact meaning of these terms in the earliest years of the colonies it is not easy to fix. They differed in size in different towns, and often in the same town. But sometimes they are all of the same or nearly the same size, and the difference only one of situation. At Barnstable they are said to have been from 6 to 12 acres, at Haverhill 5 to 22 acres, at Groton 10 to 20 acres, etc., etc. When they were of variable size in the same town, they were often proportioned to the "quality and estate" of the possessor, as at Springfield,[3] Haverhill,[4] and other places. Sometimes the right to choose a house lot was drawn for "according to estate," as at Hadley.[5]

Whatever their size or the mode of allotment, the house lots were an important part of the New England system. They were laid out so as to form a village as the centre of a plantation, and thus ensure the security of one compact settlement and the various advantages of village life. A certain dignity attached to the original lots, and it was considered important to the community that they should not be abandoned or neglected, or even thrown together.

In Connecticut, to remedy and prevent so "great an abuse," it was ordered that "all dwelling or mansion houses that are or shall be allowed in any plantation or town in this jurisdiction shall be upheld, repaired and maintained sufficient";

---

[1] Conn. Rec. I. 513.

[2] Maurer, Gesch. d. Dorfverf. I. 27.

[3] Holland, Rec. of Springfield in West Mass. I. 25.

[4] Chase, Haverhill, 56. "He that was worth £200 to have 20 acres to his lot."

[5] Judd, Hadley, etc., 287.

also, that owners of lots not built upon are to build within twelve months after date.[1]

Acre Rights or Lots.—This is an expression of entirely different nature, and merely indicates the share owned by any one in the common lands. Their value varied greatly in the different towns, but was, of course, a fixed quantity in each town. In Billerica, for instance, a 10-acre lot or right was equivalent to 113 acres of upland and 12 acres of meadow, and so on in exact proportion.[2] In Groton there were 60-acre, 20-acre, etc., rights, and there were 755 rights in all. A 60-acre right would have entitled the owner on complete partition to 3,242 acres of common lands.[3]

Pitches.—These were rights drawn in a division which entitled the drawer to lay out a lot of land in the commons wherever he might choose. The practice was common in the later history of the colonies, although not always judicially approved.

From the examination of our subject which has been made thus far, it appears that the exemption from feudal burdens in which we rejoice is not due to any merit of the colonists, for the free-socage tenure flows from the language of the grant, which, as we have seen, was not exceptional, even in England, at that day. The founders of the American colonies were not, in this respect, in advance of public sentiment in the mother country, as may be seen by reference to the journals of Parliament under James I.

But, apart from this, in every other respect the excellence of our land system is certainly due to the wisdom and patriotism of the leaders of the infant commonwealths—men who held their leadership by virtue of education, character and independent position.

The essential feature of the plan adopted in the settlement of the soil was that it was accomplished by organized col-

---

[1] Conn. Rec. I. 563.
[2] Farmer, Hist. Mem. 8.
[3] Butler, Groton, 29.

onization, and that the unit of colonization was a small plantation, which, whether from tradition or inherited, instinctive prepossession—a survival, if you will—closely resembled the ancient village communities of the Old World.

The organization of these communities and the character of the members were mainly determined by committees chosen with care by the central authority. The persons who were to compose it were selected by that authority or its committees, so that the principles of the larger commonwealth were adopted in the new settlement and carried out in the further division of the soil. Great pains were taken to guard against excessive grants and the accumulation of large estates; and the perpetual maintenance of this division into small holdings was secured by the laws of succession, while the registry laws adopted at an early date tended to the same result by making the alienation of land by deed easy and simple. Freehold tenure was the universal rule.

In the division of the soil of New England among the settlers, our ancestors were guided by no visionary theories of equality. Land, however abundant, was to be given to those who could use it. Yet no great inequality was countenanced, and every one had enough. As a rule, all the land granted was soon occupied, except the parts reserved for a time as common. In the few instances where land was allowed by non-resident holders to lie unimproved, legislation was promptly brought to bear providing for its equitable taxation, and the threatened evil was thus prevented.[1] Many grants were also by their terms made forfeitable if not improved within a given time. Provision was made for the maintenance of the ministry in all grants to communities, and the plantations generally reserved lands for school purposes.[2]

---

[1] Mass. Rec. V. 375.   A. & R. of Mass. Bay, II. 616, 941; III. 251.

[2] In New Hampshire the grants of the royal Governors reserved certain shares for public or pious uses. 10 Verm. Rep. 9. Malden was granted 1,000 acres for the use of the ministry forever; but this was exceptional. Mass. Rec., IV. Pt. II. 45.

Of scarcely less importance were the orders by which the planters were directed or encouraged to settle closely together, " for safety, Christian communion, schools, civility and other good ends." [1] The fruits of this policy are seen in the villages which form to-day so attractive and characteristic a feature of New England life.

In later days, as the settled portion of the colonies grew in extent, the forming of new plantations was sometimes left to the enterprise of leading men, and the order of the court then took a slightly different form from that which has been given.[2] But even then the purpose, conditions and exemptions of the grant are still carefully expressed in the usual terms. In New Hampshire, under the royal Governors, less care was exercised, and grants often remained unimproved for long periods. In Connecticut the action of the planters was less under the direction of the colonial authorities. Yet the general character of New England plantations was everywhere and at all periods substantially such as has been described in these pages.

Having seen how the public lands were settled and distributed among the colonists, it remains to mention briefly some of the rules of law which governed the ownership and transfer of land in the hands of private persons, and to show their adaptation to the general policy of the colonies, which has been here set forth.

The private law of real property in New England was, in the main, that of the mother country, so far as that applied to free-socage holdings. But two principles were adopted at an early day which, in the words of Chalmers, "not only mark the spirit of the people, but were, probably, the cause of most lasting consequences." [3]

The laws for the distribution of intestate estates in the colonies gave the same equal payment to all creditors, and

---

[1] Mass. Rec. V. 214.
[2] *E. g.* Mr. Thomson's grant. Mass. Rec. V. 408.
[3] MS. in possession of Mass. Hist. Soc. (cited Acts and Res. of Mass. Bay, I. 107).

(except in Rhode Island) the same equal shares to all the children, save that the eldest son received a double share. This modified preference was, not quite ingenuously, described by some of the colonies' agents as "like that of England"; but the right of primogeniture in that country was a very different thing, and the colonial rule was probably of Mosaic origin. Just as the law in England had—and has to this day—its effect upon the voluntary distribution of property by will in the custom of making "eldest sons," so the more natural provisions of colonial law encouraged the equal division of property in this country among all the children of a testator.

Laws subjecting the lands of a debtor to levy and execution, and those making the heir or executor in effect a trustee for creditors, had much to do with the prosperity of the colonies.[1] To them, says Chalmers, "much of the populousness and the commerce of Massachusetts is owing."

The transfer of land, as has been said above, was greatly facilitated by laws passed at an early day providing for the registration of titles and the simplification of conveyances, and the law thus established was substantially that which prevails at the present time.

All these rules of law, it will be seen, harmonized with the general spirit of colonial legislation, and favored the perpetuation of that order of things which the founders of New England sought by their system of settlement to produce.

For their wisdom and foresight in all these regulations respecting the disposition of public lands, and in the private law of real property, a great debt is due to them; and the more closely the causes of the prosperous social and economical condition of New England are studied, the fuller will be our appreciation of the benefits which have inured to us as the result of the land system whose foundations were laid in the early days of colonial history.

---

[1] MS. in possession of Mass. Hist. Soc. (cited Acts and Res. of Mass. Bay, I. 107).

www.ingramcontent.com/pod-product-compliance
Lightning Source LLC
Chambersburg PA
CBHW031759090426
42739CB00008B/1073